HAVING AND KEEPING

HAVING AND KEEPING

Poems by David Watts

BRICK ROAD POETRY PRESS

Cover art: Photo by wallyir at Morguefile.com

Author photo: Daphne Larkin

Library of Congress Control Number: 2017930920
ISBN-13: 978-0-9979559-1-0

Published by Brick Road Poetry Press
513 Broadway
Columbus, GA 31902-0751
www.brickroadpoetrypress.com

Brick Road logo by Dwight New

for Joan

Acknowledgments

Gratitude to these publications that first published the following poems:

Briar Cliff Review: "Pause"
The Carquinez Review: "Invisible Disgusting Things."
The Cumberland Poetry Review: "Laredo, 1945" and "Fragment at the
       Beginning of Something" (Third place winner in the Robert
       Penn Warren Poetry Contest)
International Journal of Healing and Caring: "The Body of My Brother"
Pooled Ink: "Inheritance" and "The Delicate Sprigs of Love"
Southern California Poet's Pen Newsletter: "Words," (Honorable
       Mention in the Poet's Pen Poetry Contest)
Spillway: "Empty"
The Gettysburg Review: "Na Trang" and "The Way Things Are in
       Georgetown."
Threepenny Review: "Burma Shave."
Yellow Silk: "Family Bed."

"Fragment at the Beginning of Something. . ." appeared as a
broadside collaboration with the artist Joe Dragert published by
Limestone Press in a limited edition in 1990 and was part of the
story "Annie's Antidote" in *Bedside Manners*, published by Harmony
Books, 2005.

"Inheritance" won Second Prize in the 2014 Northern
Colorado Writers Poetry Contest. "The Delicate Sprigs of Love"
was selected as the "Editor's Choice" in the same contest.
"Delicate Sprigs of Love" was also anthologized in *Written Here,
2013.*

"What it Was," "Fragment at the Beginning of Something . .
." and "The Way Things Are in Georgetown" were recorded as part
of a collaborative Jazz and Poetry CD with the Pianist and
Composer, Chris Casey in 2010.

"The Body of My Brother" was anthologized in *The Breath of Parted Lips: First Place Anthology Volume II*.

Some of the poems in this book were inspired by or modeled after the amazing work of Jack Gilbert, Jennifer K. Sweeney and Molly Bashaw.

Contents

It's the having not the keeping that is the treasure.

–Jack Gilbert

Inheritance

My father is made
of dust and intelligence.
He holds the barn together
with road signs:
Grapette, Lucky Strike,
Burma Shave,
rusty foundlings
cobbling slats together
like stitches in a fence.
He preaches Jesus.
He whistles *Turkey in the Straw.*

Mother is made from music
and culture. She bakes
bread. Opens her tilted uterus
for two sons.
She plays *Five Foot Two*
on the ukulele.
She is a long way from Laredo.

They made me
out of farming and music,
embryo
with two lines tangled,
hatched like a confounded
chicken
with a tune in its head.

So it happens the barn hums
old melodies,
names, and notes.

And the cotton rows get counted
as beats in a measure,
like Mozart,
while the combine whistles

a shed full of arias.

My father shows me harrow,
windmill, horse trough.
Already he knows my world
is different.

He knows inheritance
is like jumping through smoke.

He listens for what I hear.
The forest hums.
Even the Johnson grass squeaks
as it grows.

The Delicate Sprigs of Love

He is sitting next to her.
The firmness of her thigh is pressed against his.
There is no light between them.

He listens so heavily
into the heartbeat of her that he hears the murmuring
of aspens on the hillside.

He tells her this.
How could he sit next to her if he didn't
tell her this?

She is beautiful
in the manner in which there is so much beauty
it almost cancels itself.

I can lie down
in the golden shape of your shadow, he says,
and no longer question myself.

She wonders
if they were just prisoners of the freedom
that brought them there.

Or if to love him
would mean waiting for promises, lying awake,
in the draft of crossing stars.

They kiss
and though he is still alone in the fear that no one will ever
        kiss him
he is sitting next to her.

Broken Jar

The heart wanders
then it questions itself.
Pleasure, then the horror
of guns and tanks in Syria.
We'd rather ghazals
in moonlight. The turn of a face
as she disappears around
the corner. The desire for peace
while war runs its poison
alongside. Each morsel
of tranquility more precious
as memory chimes in
with hot Louisiana days,
lemonade, and mother
at the piano. I'd like to think
what memory wants us
to think, sitting securely
on its fence post
lifting particles of light
from the broken jar.
But the world is beyond us
even as we live inside it—
The sun comes and goes.
The moon breathes and circles us
with reflected light,
while the soul holds the body
carefully in its arms
as we walk through the perforated dark.

Words

My father used few words.
He moved fearless
from task to task as if
they were meals to be eaten.
Our house grew inglenooks
from the imagination of the carpenter
he became.

From tree limbs of summer
I watched him tote
and saw, driving nails
with the same muscles
that lost baseballs
over West Texas outfields.

Leaves turned.
Snow fell.
All that whiteness
came. Standing
in the emptiness of transition
he spoke
imploring wisdom.
Then, when the inkwell went dry
he reached with great and somber hands
to turn out the light.

Offenbach's Barcarolle

He wondered why he chose
what he chose to remember,
his mother playing Barcarolle
on the piano—
the sad arrangement of notes
that made his tummy go wonky—not
remembering her practicing,
every perfect note a performance.

He remembers the girl
down the alleyway who told him
adding soap to Kool-Aid
was a way to expand
the taste. Her soft eyes.
He'd believe anything she said.

Cardboard boxes he made
into houses his cats wouldn't
live in. The rich blossoming
of wisteria. Prunes
he tried to feed the dog. Learning
that longing glances
don't mean what they seem.

The weather freakish enough
for snow in Texas.
Drivers insane with laughter
sliding into the ditch. The boy
thinking this life was
the one life
he would always lead, mother
at the kitchen table,
dad tinkering in the tool shed,
the strains of Barcarolle
in his brain.

Burma Shave

Crescent of soap
in the dish, absence
where the brushstrokes
brushed, weeks
like that, and then my wife brings
this new cake—Burma Shave,
new lather, old idea,
the way road signs
could be broken
into chains of small
crosses,
aphorisms that went down
in pieces,
a barber who
could make his tie wiggle,
eyes go wall-eyed—little tricks
derived from enough time
and resource to entertain,
facials, boot black,
something of color
in a bottle that splashed
when you shook it,
orange blossom, rose
water, the men
in their shirts, their short
hair, characters
who wouldn't know
the play had finished its run
but for this new cake
in my dish,
its aroma, its texture,
its name against my skin.

I Tie Knots in the Strings of Memory

and tighten them against forgetting.
They cannot imitate her hungry look,
eyes glazed, lips parted, but they prevent
imperfect forgetting. With my fingers
I choose what I own of the past,
arranging flashes of light
the way a movie wants to be told,
part accuracy, part fiction,
part what the body wants to keep
of its bumblings in this world,
late at night when it pans the past
for gold, the lines tangling and un-
tangling in the swift undertow
of the strong passing current.

Creekside at Smith's Branch

Along some creeksides
twists of stone lie

among the shale
and the lime, like secrets

a girlfriend wants to tell—
ammonite, trilobite,

toothpaste squirts
with a frozen history. My horse,

old but spunky, I ride hard
against the hills and banksides.

Needing rest and grazing
we spread a blanket of hours

in which I play geologist, absorbing
evidence like globes of light

shining on old texts.
Doesn't everyone want to know

what is permanent in this world?
I thought I knew, yet one night

beyond this low water bridge,
a girlfriend made love

to another man. Permanence, then,
nothing more than a teen-age

illusion, dissolving in creek water—
car lights down, the night sky

hemorrhaging, the little fossils
inconsolable in their powdery beds.

Another Side of Transgression

He thought of all the time he wasted
being good. Clutched by the guilt
of excellence. Polite.
Well-trained. But when
the long summer afternoons came,
too hot to move
from the window fan, scent
of vapor rising
from water jackets, he found pleasure
in doing the nothing that had no regrets—
wasted afternoons
under the Wisteria vine when no one
was watching. Aroma thick
as a breeze on his shoulder.
Thinking of women constantly, forgetting
to water the chickens
in the barn. He was beginning to feel
the release of duty, to feel
what it's like to feel.
Demands waiting like barking dogs
at the periphery. His good intention
to visit the sick woman
falling aside
as he listened to the rattle of starlings
in the rafters—discovering that strange lightness
of the body. And the new importance
of oak branches
where they separate from the trunk.
How far out the leaves
begin to spread.
The startling arrangement
of moss
like whiskers without discipline.
The long plains of earth

reaching to the clouds
behind the back yard fence.
How the ground pushes back when you walk.

Na Trang

My brother straps on his webbing, his belt,
his canteen, sidearm . . . gone
are the colors he was—blue jeans,

white shirt, sweet potato skin—
he is so deep in camouflage
even his blue eyes

are like cinders. He climbs
to his bunker,
mushroom of concrete and divots,

ear to a shortwave
that sneezes facts and lies
that no one can remember,

each moment of cigarettes and coffee
possibly the last. Nothing
could have prepared him for this . . .

. . . death little more
than the morning news.
Something happened to him there.

I don't know what it was but
it taught him how to leave this life
real easy, bowing to the side

to let the train he was riding
pass on by. After that,
death was just another order to obey,

flat, like a paper command,
a switch to turn off the static
they jammed down his ear.

The Body of My Brother

First it belonged to my mother
or seemed to
stuffed into her
like a foot in a sock.
Then it took care of itself
filling out
into home runs, high jumps.
There were times
it must have been afraid
hiding in a bunker
in South Viet Nam
having happen to it whatever it was
that makes bodies years later
leap out of bed in the middle of the night
not awake
sweating and shouting . . .
Last time I saw it
it was older than mine
thinned out
by too many cigarettes
and favors given.
Now they've taken it
from the hospital bed
where it gasped out its last punch line
and put it in a box
that no one will ever see again,
though we stand around it
observing gestures even death cannot remove:
head tilt, wry smile,
hands the same as my hands
crossed over his chest
as they never were in life,
a few pictures and mementos
scattered around it, as if
they were crumbs of a happy life.

by David Watts from
Having and Keeping
Brick Road Poetry Press
©2017

Pleasure

Because she felt pleasure
running like that,
the speed faster,
the tight muscles tight
where the waist
curves its sharp turn
curving,
the hip moving,
the thigh
moving . . .

Because she said the word
pleasure
he was there
with his imaginary eyes,
imaginary hands
where the waist
makes its tight
turn, the hip
moving, the thigh moving . . . because

she said the word he remembered
pleasure remains
in the world
despite sorrows,
living on by the imagination.

Who should refuse beauty,
then,
when it blows its rare blessing
our way . . .
speaking in the voice

of this quick running,
the tight curves,

the excitement
even she didn't know she could feel . . . ?

That is why when he thinks
of her
he will always
think of her out there
on the trail
running, flushed
and fair.

Man at the Window

He stands at the window baffled
by pleasure and how brief it is.
Pleasure followed by the memory
of pleasure. Light
then dark with a splinter
left in. Something like that.
The woman in the chair is reading,
drinking tea in the ground glass
haze of evening.
The sudden swell he feels
watching her
illuminates the past she spent
getting to this place:
a lover who left, perhaps. Time
setting her kitchen in order, or maybe
gathering artichokes from the field.
The moment opens in a diorama
of impermanence, seeping away
at the edges even as it is breathed
into vision the first time. He holds out
his arms. He wants this moment
in the body, to feel there
the pleasure it holds, and then
whatever it is that pleasure
leaves behind,
which is all he can keep.
The strange quality of light
dissolving like smoke in air,
slipping away
in the sun's diminishing gaze.

Things My Son Told Me

for Gabriel

Dad, I like you . . . I don't kiss you very much
because you shave a lot.

I have a badly good flaming hot mechanical voice.

You know what's interesting?
You can run your finger through fire without getting burned
but you can't run your finger through water without getting wet.

The crossing guard had an item of despair
in which his soul was contained.

Hey dad, did you know that the more you grow the less smart you
        get?

I'm 8 years old, immature, courageous and awesome.

Remind me why I'm getting up today.

We Come Upon a Clearing at Evening

The rain off the Pacific slashes the split-rail fence and presses against the moraine. The valley is wider. The sedges older.

I wish you were here to see this.

The Colorado trips we took, kids and food and gear in the station wagon, all of us searching for manifestations of beauty . . .

Here there is a different beauty. The wind swells, the Tanager lifts to the pine— each rising like a spirit ascending against the weight of loss. Wood and bone and patches of lichen. The Tanager will go and the tree remain. What is the meaning of survival if we are left behind?

Standing against this wind I can feel the absence that beauty contains.

This poem will finish when it wants to. But it will not have answers. Poetry only asks the questions. Maybe we can hope for a metaphor, some crisp phrase to explain how beauty can live with grace alongside grief.

The rain has passed Emigrant Peak, climbing thrusts of granite on its way to the plains. It is done with us. I should have been there for your death.

Something Arrives That Slows the Moment

He wondered if love was possible
so far away from satisfaction.
The luster of love transparent
as a shadow on a moving curtain. But then,

he found himself alongside the Potomac
seated at a small round table,
opposite a beautiful woman,
the early evening arriving
on a soft breeze
crossing the terrace, her eyes
his alone—

he was certain if he trembled
the illusion would shatter.

The sun glistened
across the speeding waters,
its long orange arm grasping the earth
in a last moment of departure.
The important conversation
about unimportant things would not
be remembered
but for the frantic dance
around a maypole
that stood for something intimate.

Shocking how easy, he thought,
when easy
turns your way.
Makes lies of the past
and a saint of dreaming.

The moment, meanwhile, had stalled,
unwilling to be pulled
into the sprockets of time,

a brief hesitation that allowed him to hold on
to the sweetness of it
while the parenthesis he couldn't identify
tied the moment down,
long enough to realize
now that he knew what was possible
he would be hungry forever.

Invisible Disgusting Things

When we fell out of love
all the disgusting things
I'd never noticed woke up
and started bothering me:

the empty spool of paper
on the roll, the late
car payments, the way
the soap goes gushy

in the dish. Love hid them
for years in full view
lying around like shapes
without pigment.

Now they rub against me
in the night,
and mix with things
we talk about when we talk.

Conversations bloat
like spoiled fish. Hard truths
grind like tired bones
now that love has gone.

Empty

Walls and a floor. Five pots
in the cupboard. He didn't mind
the furniture missing. That
could change. The other missings
he couldn't fix. He watched
as the fear of loneliness
changed places with loneliness.
Even so, he didn't die. *Breathe deeply*, he said.
Laugh self-reflectively. He went outside
to feel the wind moving.
Throw a stone. Touch a tree. Saturday
noticed there was laundry
piled in the corner. Strange pleasure, watching
the comforting gesture of clothes
tumbling in the dryer. Little drudgeries
finding their way in the new order.
Sparkles of unexplained joy
where they weren't supposed to be:
Balancing the checkbook. Washing
three dishes and a spoon.
Apple slices and Bordeaux cookies
after dinner. Miles Davis on the one
small radio.
Things began to settle. A bit.
But when the children didn't show on Christmas,
the dark half of him wagged its finger
and said, *I told you so.*
The other half, clinging to a belief in grace,
was shocked how easily his history
could be erased. Loss
made itself larger then, darting
among the unclaimed gifts
lined with care against the wall.
And he saw
how the passageway to the future

had narrowed.
Nod wisely, he said.
Fold your hands.
Say thank you, please.

After Long Silence Running into
My Ex at a Family Gathering

It was not about sorrow,
though a newspaper did blow
across a darkened road,

and we got helplessly lost
on the way to the Bat Mitzvah.
Sorrow would have been easier

than its recovery
and that stone-hard certainty
that loss waits at the end of the sentence.

It was about the fragile cellophane
between decorum
and a deathly swan dive. The screech

held back, the coiled
spring not sprung, tense and unforgiving,
the son we destroyed

not even there.

Pause

All day in shelter
on a granary floor, rain
on the roof like buckshot
in branches. Aroma
of wet earth, dry
grain. The air unhurried
and intentional. I have made
a chair of hay bales, spread
a saddle blanket. Contained
womb-like against the heft
of the out-of-doors, there is
this soft heartbeat of contentment.
The dark print of my life
outside the walls.

More Gabrielisms

I don't like those Root Beer Pez.
They taste like static.

I'm going to draw a cat with a cranky face . . .
with eyes like these, you know he's up to something.

If you look at the moon and shake your head, it turns loops.

Dad, I think there's something wrong with my bottom.
It's not doing its job.
The hole there stays shut and then it opens.
Yeah. I think it's reading the daily news right now.

Disobey the other parts of your body
but always listen to your heart and your lungs.

I know what I'm doing and I do what I know.
That's an old saying I like.
And I just made it up.

The Woman

The woman is a memory to him
but not a presence. What scoops
from the embrace they made
is how their bodies briefly
were unafraid.
How for an instant they dipped
close to joy. Memory turns
its direction and hides
what it wants to hide,
but sometimes it splashes
a clothesline with a white
flag of remembrance.
They couldn't have planned
that flag
but it got there somehow,
beginning the moment he gestured
and she fell against him.
Simple, like that.
Almost a swoon. Words
not necessary when the spirit
wants to move. Now
a particle of those three seconds
glows behind consciousness
like gold under water, shimmering
if you're close enough to see it.
Eyes lit with hunger, chasing
what was lost.

Affair

He didn't know how it started
but he did know that inside
the pleasure was a loneliness
he could not fill.
He came for the bed-mate
but was given a companion, one
who opened her door
every time he asked. She made
the emptiness under his ribcage
go away. They knew
they could not last
so they were allowed
to bring the best they had and place it
on the kitchen table, time
too scarce for the crankiness
of long years, the clock slowing
its hands, the bonsai in the window
beautiful in its narrow soil.

The Woman I Loved in Mountains

was not the woman she was
twenty years before, nor was I
what I was. Which is good.

We should not have been first lovers.

Only by this ripening
could we be penetrated
with pleasure enough
to last this long.

My molecules replace themselves
in a few years
yet I am called by the same name.
I love the same woman
though she, too, has changed.

We are not the castle but the ghosts
in its rooms. Consciousness
not my electrons spinning
but the smoke from the fires
they burn, rising.

What holds me in place
is not my name or what I do
but what I love.
And what loves me.

The woman from mountains
sits across the table.
She holds a spoon in her delicate
hand. The light from the open window
that illuminates her
has never been in this world before.

What it Was

for Duston

And they asked if it felt like sex
when the sperm hit the egg.
And I said no, which was true, partly,
the in-body sex and the out-
of-body sex—

But they weren't talking biology.

She explained it like conversation,
the egg mother did:
she said she had come to believe
in benevolence, honored
to be chosen, asked me
to give the shot that would start her eggs
rolling, and I did—brief exposure
on a different bed—clinical touch,
fluids entering.

Distance fenestrated, but kept.

—well it did and it didn't
feel like sex, and a child grew
where sex was still trying
to make up its mind.
And the mother who wombed
this child
wondered if sex would be different
now,
new presence claiming the ache
where absence used to be.

Well maybe. And meanwhile
he grew, this child,
and was intelligent, and how
openly his mother could brag

about him, someone said,
because she felt no genetic
connection. What did I know?

I thought it would be the same,
though
it's not the same, is it?—
the womb space connection
and the egg space
connection?—a distinction by truth
and the memory of loss.

Well, they asked again, is it sex
when it happens in a Petri dish?
And I told them the story

Steven Dunn tells,
the girl's poem about making love
in a boat.
A boy in her class said it wasn't
love,
it was fucking.
She said
if it felt like love, it was.
And I say

two women sit on a bed
exchanging poems—
two wombs, one egg—
the one egg missing, the one
provided—

they are writing about the child
and I am in a different room
making myself into
background.

And did I tell you the part
about the boy sitting
in the lavatory this morning?

dipping his washcloth in water—

to make him warm, he said—
draping his legs, almost floating
in his steamy containment?

And the little strings
and beads of water falling
on the tiles
in necklaces of abundance,
and I tell you it is
whatever it wants to be,
sex, love, lust,
benevolence . . .

this waterchild, this miracle,
this family.

Family Bed

Now we make love around
a baby
morsel of flesh
in the bed between us
pray for sleep we say
and not waking
and he did that for us
asleep but not
unconscious
for when you rose along the long shelf
to come
he followed your breath marks
with his
heave and sigh
stuttering in his sleep
and in the cup
where the body loses its containment
he made your sound
for you
your gasp
your choked sigh
your breathless grateful undoing.

Heat and Language

for Duston

Heat today. Smell
of creekbed, of water
where it used to run.

I said, *Monarch,*
and my son said, *orange
butterfly.*

I said, *kitty-cat-mailbox.*
And he said, *meow-meow.*
What is it they say, the farther

words are from the source
the less we feel? His
closer than mine. Yesterday

she said, *Do you suppose
the egg mother will want to avoid
the child?* And I wondered

if she was thinking of shots
and pelvic exams, the transfer
of something unnamable. What

was it like, the egg
inside the needle, the sperm
surrounding?

Like sex? Like dying?
She could have her reasons
for staying away—too much

separation in the close proximity.
It was Bull Creek, the smell
of August rising

lifting where the creek
had spent itself, organic, like estrus
before the whispering embryo—

her creek bed, I thought,
my water—some things
we feel but do not say.

Yet underneath this language
there grows a little family,
a little cluster of eggs.

Moss drying, stone drying,
there are four of us
though we are only three.

Gabrielisms III

(Falling asleep in the back of the car . . .)
Dad, everywhere you go I want to go.

Dad, do we have any inferior human food?

A dream is basically an entertainment system.

You end up in the time continuum.
You can go anywhere from there. And I think you can
know everything. You can understand time and get out 25
years later. You can go how fast you want.
Really?
Yes and I am so good at physics.

I remember things behind things.

(Gabriel leaves a message on our phone talking like Arnold
Schwarzenegger:)
Hello. This is God.
I would like to have a party at your house.
So, can I bring Jesus?
And come to have the popcorn and the candy, yah?
And the movie?
And maybe some chips on dips? Yah Boy. . .
Time to go to sleep, Gabriel.
I can't, it's illegal in California.

Trying to Write This Poem

There is a finch on a branch
inside me that has a song
he's not singing. I woke up

thinking of her at Squaw Valley
where we were alone
among strangers, then

at Waterloo where
I was learning how her friends
talk to each other.

Time holds moments
it wants to remember. But the finch
twitters and does not sing.

What is it about beauty? How it
falls from the shoulders of women
who wear it like a summer shawl?

Passion not a color, a fire
in a bottle and silence
underneath it all. But

the finch is still there, hovering
in that silence, and my poem
is running around naked

but for what memory will allow,
dropping like shooting stars
in this chasm between intention

and actually writing a poem.
And the bird looks at me
like I'm finally getting it.

Blue Norther

When the wind comes back
over the North Pole

it lifts the grackles
from their gnarly tree like flakes
of black confetti.

From there
they fly inside me

and I run into the turbulence
of the Norther's edge,
wings flapping,
no longer a creature of the ground.

The flesh of its dark
leading edge is an ear
I speak to—
pocket full of questions—

as midnight's cloak
snuffs the sun
before crossing the knife edge
of noon.

Block of ice on wheels,
rocket
exploding
among fragments of air.

Soundless snow comes now,
a kingdom no one possesses.

As the sticky air lies in splinters
on the ground

I am inside, toasting my astonished feet
over the floor furnace,

branches of spidery inks
gone powdery in the snow,
the air cracking,
my blood brimming.

Virus

The sun is a fried egg.
The wind has a door in it
I walk through.

In the dark below my molecules
there is a vibration
that makes no sound.

And the earth under my feet
is held together
by silence.

The doctor smiled an archaic smile
which means I will spend 2015
getting over 14.

Mother spent a lot of time,
I now remember, in bed. Maybe her gene
bewitches me.

My body so careful it stops
at railroads.
The flesh engaged, the spirit darting.

Now even love is filled with such longing
it hums in the night
as I rise to the promise of your touch.

Perfection

The woman in black has no breasts.
Her spine pushes through her skin
like a brontosaurs erupting
from its tar pit. Her backside
sloughs like road melt.
She is entering the caldron
of the Stairmaster to burn
creases between her muscles.

The woman in yellow has nice
breasts, tight hips, and a little pot
for a belly. She is lifting weights
to put roundness, in the right
proportions, in the right
places. She wants some
of what the woman in black has,
but not all. Both are reaching

beyond reaching,
as the on-lookers they desire
but do not want, pass by. The woman
in black avoids my gaze,
the woman in yellow the same,
while their bodies contort and obey
and wait to be loved.

Laredo, 1945

Mums is sleeping.
All the sentences she diagrammed
are falling out of her mouth:

the impossible one
from *'Twas the Night
Before Christmas* even she

wasn't sure about.
It is summer.
South Texas. Afternoon.

Heat rises
off the red clay
like bad breath.

Only the window is cool.
The fan, relentless,
lifts her lacy collar

as it strokes the room.
I am five years old.
Already her goiter

is visible to me
snapped to her neck
like a turtle.

Pops is sleeping
in the tool
shed, his nails sorted

in fruit jars nailed
to the two-by-two, army knife
strung to a belt loop.

They are snoring,
singing to each other
from their places.

The Way Things Are in Georgetown

Even the courthouse didn't know
where he was buried. She asked
if I wanted a copy of his death
certificate. But I said I knew
he was dead. I just wanted to know
where. It was the day before

Thanksgiving, near noon, mother
in the hospital, and my options
were running out. Something about
getting dad buried without a headstone
was good enough at the time.
And then the money

ran out, or—the concept returned
it was okay for middle class families
not to finish things.
The lady said the funeral home might know—
they didn't, but they knew who did. I never
would have guessed.
It was Parks and Recreation
in the new building north

of the north branch of the San Gabriel River. So,
I went in with the basketball players
who reminded me of all the reasons why
I never played basketball, and the young
women about to go swimming who
reminded me of . . .

and the woman said, *Sure, Honey. It would be
in the file cabinet behind the summer
baseball schedules*, and she brought out
the map and pointed to plot number 51.
And I went there, and stood a long time
under the great sycamore tree.

Re-Vision:

Starting with a line from Jack Gilbert

He watches the music with his eyes closed.
In a dark room inhabited by the imagination.
Sounds enter him like a request offered
but forgotten, a present
his mother might have ordered
from Sears and Roebuck
that surprised everyone when it arrived.
He lets the music occupy him
the way a new lover
moves everything to one side.
Now every vibration is a vibration
of possibility. Order
imagines itself in the chaos
of everybody talking. And he hears
how music connects back, how
it anchors memory
where it wants to slide away into darkness:
The high school dance where *Stairway*
to Heaven was playing.
His cross-country travel
while Dylan sang *Lay Lady Lay*.
The girl he met listening to Elvis
on the beach at Indiana Dunes
who kept hiking up
her bathing suit and repeating, *Texas*
is the wide-open state.
The girl is gone. The dance is over.
Dylan is doing other things and the sounds
have found a circular path
that is almost permanent.
Everything matters, when suddenly in floodlight
against the dark of forgetting.
Notes and silence in between.
Sounds in the street and the heart
open. Jupiter moaning

like a guard dog and the imprint
somehow manages to stay alive
where memory has attached its kite string
to make it dance.

Trying to Leave the Marriage

He finds out where the dream will take him
by destroying the previous dream.
The heart shy to the carnage
it takes to find the heart,

shy to the courage to redefine
the morning light. He stands at a window
watching his children playing in the yard, worrying
what the neighbors will think when he leaves

as he has worried years before, closing the cage
against the pathway of his heart.
There is so little time.
We must insist, he thinks. We must accept

disaster as permission for tendrils of growth
under the canopy of an uncontrolled burn.
Even in the sinking moments sure to come
when the dark invades the empty apartment

in the low rent district, among the clatter
of lost pleasures and torn ideas,
there might be buried within that suffering
a different kind of morning.

Gabrielisms IV

Graffiti is just a language almost no one understands.

It's so mysterious how you can see a dot or a mark on a tree.
It's like someone lay down under the tree and sunk into the ground.
Like maybe he died there and went down into the roots.
Like you see a knot for two eyes . . .

Hey Dad. You know what's really neat? The brain can project this
thing on your skull called the imagination. It's like a little picture
show. Yeah, and you can actually be in it.

When I stop all my thoughts all these chips float around in my
            brain.
Yeah, chips. They come forward and turn to me. Thought chips.
Oh, you know, night muse, daydreams, things I want to do, habits.
I can pick one and play it.
It's the new chip that's really hard to control sometimes.

Hey, Dad. Did you know the golf ball goes farther if you speak to
            it
in more than one language?
What languages do you speak to it in?
Japanese and Spanish.
Japanese, really? What do you say?
Sayonara amigo ball.

I've discovered that the Chinese worry balls don't take away the
            fear.
They just take away the worry about the fear.
If I say to myself, I'm afraid of dying the fear is still there
but the worry about the fear is gone.

I have a gift for Ethan. Coffee Creamers,
Bubble Yum and Coca-Cola Pez.
It's 10 year-old heaven, Dad. Get used to it.

Dad? What would you want regarding staying the same age?
For me it's 9. Stay the same size, same weight . . .
Only develop more skills . . .
Actually, I wouldn't want that.
What do you want then?
One of those motorcycle things.

I'm not afraid of death.
A lot of people are but I'm not.
It's part of life.
It's like the last page in a book.

Did you know that the spirit is the most powerful thing in the
        body?
It controls the heart and the lungs and the electricity.
And when you die it can open a brick wall.

I can see things when I know where they are.

Rita's Kiss

We'd like to think what happens in the dark
is real, that shadow
is just the light's rearrangement of a difficult truth.

—split fragment

Rita almost kissed me when the lights
went out. I was thirteen.
She thought about it, but chickened out.
Her telling me later was the offering
of a gift I didn't get. Flooded, then,
by the immensity of what I'd lost,
my heartache made me want her
all the more, want her
to try again, lips searching the dark behind
a cooperative light switch. I was way too timid
to ask. The dark, porous only briefly
to the release of desire, closed
when the lights came back on.
The opportunity missed
would not have been so painful
if not announced.
But she announced. Excitement
and disappointment the virtues we shared
like jam on stale toast.
Some might say we were cubs
playing at the pale reflection of love, too young
for it to mean much more. But her kiss,
not given,
made us spectators of ourselves,
the watched image the only part of it
that was true. Silence came then.
And the air moved like the sludge of sorrow
when all I had of her was a little light, a little dark,
and just the idea of her kiss.

Fragment at the Beginning of Something . . .

My son brings me a stone and asks
which star it fell from. He is serious
and so I must be careful,
even though I know he will place it
among those things that will leave him
someday, and he will go on, gathering.
For this is one of those moments
that turns suddenly toward you, opening
as it turns, as if for an instant
we paused on the edge of a heartbeat
and then pressed forward, conscious
of the fear that runs beside us
and how lovely it is to be with each other
in the long resilient mornings.

Family Away, Empty House

The house was suddenly empty
and he wondered how
Aunt Phyl managed to live alone
after Eula Lee died.
All that space.
No one in it.
What came to him then
was, *You do what you have to do,*
as if she'd heard and answered.

Alone now with his new disease,
new pills, the edge of the universe
closer, he wondered
what life would be like without him
as he cleared dishes
from the table, folded clothes
from the dryer—a covenant
of affection for common tasks.

Two kinds of emptiness, he thought,
the one with, the other without
him. Everything precious
and not so precious any more:
the cannonball
shot over the Rio Grande
during the Mexican-American War,
the Ansel Adams photograph,
his record collection from the Sixties.
His grip upon them unfolding
even as they drifted
from him. The unknown world
he'd wanted to understand
so much nearer.

What would he keep from this world?

Summer heat in the mountains,
a woman's laughter across
the plaza, the surprise of her bright greeting
as she pulled him from the terrible cold.

Longevity

Thinking how I've outlived
my father and my mentor
by the same number of years,
youth gone and death
not finding me. The summer
hypnotic, buzzing its way toward
winter. Drone of airplanes
in the heated air. There is this intimate
loneliness drifting among the redwoods.
Astounded my clock still ticking
since thinking long ago everything
was already good enough. My children
spread like buckets of water
splashed upon a granary floor. That same
wide radius I once made,
my family decades behind me,
the telephone ring
quiet. I celebrate
this moment, its diminuendos of light
and architecture,
my mind thinking of peace, my body,
of nothing.

The Gift of the Commonplace

She is downstairs working
on her manuscript, or maybe
her promotion to full professor—I'm
not sure. This moment of ordinariness
will be forgotten between moments
when she lies close to me in bed
and opens herself to my nervous heart,
or between that moment
when I first heard her laugh
across a room full of people
and when I heard the cries
of our newborn children. What I want
is not just the riverstones
we polish with our thumbs
and place in a glass on the mantle,
but what happens between
the things we remember—
like how it is to feel
her unspoken presence within the house.
Ordinary,
the matrix we stand upon.
She will finish and come
upstairs. The space between
my knowing and her arrival
I will remember.

Having and Keeping

She takes off her clothes without reservation.
The territories of her body sing
the sweet harmonies that are particular
to her. How the cave
of her navel, the valleys between ribs
know to love each other.

If I am lucky, I will be allowed
to enter the heart of this woman and wrap
her body around me
before sorrow returns, and she
has moved on to someone else.

The moment with this woman, if it happened,
is gone. Things are not what they were.
The hot wind off a Texas prairie, a family
touring Colorado in a green and beige
nineteen-fifty-three Chevy wagon
might have happened too. One cannot be sure.
Having is different from keeping.

My daughter sends an email from Connecticut.
She is happy about the music the grandchildren
are making. The beauty of what I hear
has left their voices
and they are off washing dishes or doing
homework. What I am listening to is a memory
of where they were when they made this music.

I look across my deck to the arrangement
of branches against the setting sun.
The woodpecker's red tuft glints perfectly
in the fading light. What I see
has changed even

before the woodpecker flies away.
I cannot keep where he was or anything else
about him.

But if these things happened,
even in approximation to what I believe,
then I have been given this music, the vacation,
the hot wind off the prairie and maybe
even the woman.
It is enough to think so.

How to Survive the Cold

Do not succumb to winter. Do not
let the north wind
sink its cold teeth in your body
and cross the heated wall
of your blood. Shovel a path

to the storm cellar. Take down
with the lava red glow
of raspberries. Open it. Inhale
the sunny nectars of August.

Gather wood from the shed. Winter
is only waiting for you
to build your fire. Cook skillet
scones on the grate. Kernel of wheat,

baking powder, cream
of tartar. Buttermilk, well shaken.
Cook undisturbed.
Let your sweetbutter melt
deep into the bread's yellow heart.
Prop your feet to the fire.

When the afternoons quicken
unhook the rope and pulley down
the quilt in its frame, the one
you were working on last
winter. Sew in April.
Sew in haystacks, Beethoven,
Brahms.
And when your hands grow tired,

blow out the lantern
and tell your grandmother's stories
over again.

There will be windfall apples
in the pantry, half-moons
you cut and dried in October's
hesitant sun. And before you forget,
set out the seed
for the winterbird.

Then settle for the long evening.
Read a poem. Sing a hymn.
How many years has spring listened
for your distant song?

About the Author

David Watts grew up in Texas, thus the scattered references throughout this work to the characteristics of the terrain and subtle tonalities that capture the personalities of the people there. The "can do" attitude that characterized his family helped him to move forward into many fields, medicine, classical music, scientific invention, radio and television hosting and production, and finally, after mid-life, to become a poet and a writer.

His literary credits include seven books of poetry, two collections of short stories, a mystery novel, a best-selling western and several essays. He has received awards in academics, medical excellence, television production and for the quality of his writing. He is a Clinical Professor of Medicine at the University of California San Francisco and Professor of Poetry at the Fromm Institute at the University of San Francisco. He lives in California with his wife and two sons.

BRICK ROAD
POETRY PRESS

Our Mission

The mission of Brick Road Poetry Press is to publish and promote poetry that entertains, amuses, edifies, and surprises a wide audience of appreciative readers. We are not qualified to judge who deserves to be published, so we concentrate on publishing what we enjoy. Our preference is for poetry geared toward dramatizing the human experience in language rich with sensory image and metaphor, recognizing that poetry can be, at one and the same time, both familiar as the perspiration of daily labor and as outrageous as a carnival sideshow.

Also Available from Brick Road Poetry Press

www.brickroadpoetrypress.com

POETRY PRESS

Also Available from Brick Road Poetry Press

www.brickroadpoetrypress.com

Dancing on the Rim by Clela Reed

Possible Crocodiles by Barry Marks

Pain Diary by Joseph D. Reich

Otherness by M. Ayodele Heath

Drunken Robins by David Oates

Damnatio Memoriae by Michael Meyerhofer

Lotus Buffet by Rupert Fike

The Melancholy MBA by Richard Donnelly

Two-Star General by Grey Held

Chosen by Toni Thomas

Lauren Bacall Shares a Limousine by Susan J. Erickson

Ambushing Water by Danielle Hanson

About the Prize

The Brick Road Poetry Prize, established in 2010, is awarded annually for the best book-length poetry manuscript. Entries are accepted August 1st through November 1st. The winner receives $1000 and publication. For details on our preferences and the complete submission guidelines, please visit our website at www.brickroadpoetrypress.com.

CPSIA information can be obtained
at www.ICGtesting.com
Printed in the USA
BVHW071441220419
546167BV00002B/453/P

9 780997 955910